THE FIRST ESSAY

ON

The Political Rights of Women

A Translation of Condorcet's Essay
"Sur l'admission des femmes au droit de Cité"
(On the Admission of Women to the Rights of
Citizenship)

Dr. Alice Vickery Drysdale (1844–1929), Translator

BY

DR. ALICE DRYSDALE VICKERY

(WITH PREFACE AND REMARKS)

LETCHWORTH:

GARDEN CITY PRESS LIMITED

PREFACE

More than one hundred years have passed away since, in 1789, the Marquis de Condorcet wrote his "Esquisse sur l'Admission des Femmes au Droit de Cité," and yet the problem of women's enfranchisement still awaits an equitable solution. Those of us who are old enough to remember the inauguration of the popular movement for the extension of the franchise to women (which may be dated from the day in which our late noble leader, JOHN STUART MILL, addressed the House of Commons on this subject, in May, 1867), feel that our lives are passing away while wearily awaiting the dilatory educational development of mankind in this question.

John Stuart Mill (1806–1873), Pioneer of Women's Freedom

The essential principles of our claim have been reiterated again and again. We form one-half of the human race, and need recognition by the law as much as the other half of the race. But, as long as our law-makers are not directly responsible to us for their conduct in Parliament, they may, and do, safely neglect our interests, and pass laws which jeopardise our liberties and subordinate our just rights of person, property, and offspring to the supposed interests of the men whom they represent.

The spirit which animates Parliament pervades the whole of our social life; and women suffer from lack of educational facilities, and from obstacles to success in industrial and professional life, in ways which have no parallel in the case of men. All these things have been urged again and again until we are weary of repeating them; and we ask ourselves, as we mentally review our position, Where shall we find some new argument wherewith to arrest the attention, and compel the action, of those who have the power, but seem to lack the will, to do justice? It is curious to note that the great point on which the mass of men seem united is theirsex. Prejudices of race, of caste, of colour may be overcome; but the pride of sex remains. Rights of citizenship are accorded to the small shopkeeper, artisan, lodger, agricultural labourer, and to the illiterate who knows no difference between one party and the other, either as to tendencies or methods of government. The Anglo-Saxon confers rights of citizenship upon the foreigner, upon the negro (as in the United States), upon the Maori (as in New Zealand)--the last of whom, sitting in the New Zealand House of Representatives, helped to maintain this glorious prerogative of sex by giving their casting-votes against a measure intended to meet the claims of the Anglo-Saxon women in New Zealand.[1]

And all this despite the admitted fact that the social and economic problems, which are coming more and more into the field of parliamentary labours, are all but incapable of solution without the help of enfranchised women.

Must women, then, following the example of men, learn to put sex in the first place and regard all other interests as secondary? Is this really what men wish to force women to do? One would think not. At present women have not adopted any such principle of action. They are divided rather than otherwise, according to the relations they occupy with regard to men. The married woman, on the one hand, seems opposed to the claims of the widowed and single, on the other--andvice versâ; and both together combine to ostracise some of their own sex. It seems probable, however, that we women will have to learn to drop all such rivalries, and determine to form one vast organisation, which shall include within its ranks all sorts and conditions of women, and shall extend over the whole of the United

Kingdom, if we would not see this nineteenth century completed without Woman's Emancipation becoming an accomplished fact.

[1]The Parliamentary Franchise was conferred on the women of New Zealand in 1893, the same year in which the above was printed. In 1907 the Hon. R. Oliver, late member of the Legislative Council, writes: "The interest now taken by women in New Zealand in the politics of the country is remarkable, and is regarded as a decided gain to the community."

Suffragettes campaigning for Votes for Women, early 20th century

ON THE ADMISSION OF WOMEN TO THE RIGHTS OF CITIZENSHIP

BY THE MARQUIS DE CONDORCET

Marie Jean Antoine Nicolas de Caritat, Marquis de Condorcet (1743–1794)

Custom may familiarise mankind with the violation of their natural rights to such an extent, that even among those who have lost or been deprived of these rights, no one thinks of reclaiming them, or is even conscious that they have suffered any injustice.

Certain of these violations (of natural right) have escaped the notice of philosophers and legislators, even while concerning themselves zealously to establish the common rights of individuals of the human race, and in this way to lay the foundation of political institutions. For example, have they not all violated the principle of the equality of rights in tranquilly depriving one-half of the human race of the right of taking part in the formation of laws by the exclusion of women from the rights of citizenship? Could there be a stronger proof of the power of habit, even among enlightened men, than to hear invoked the principle of equal rights in favour of perhaps some 300 or 400 men, who had been deprived of it by an absurd prejudice, and forget it when it concerns some 12,000,000 women?

To show that this exclusion is not an act of tyranny, it must be proved either that the natural rights of women are not absolutely the same as those of men, or that women are not capable of exercising these rights.

But the rights of men result simply from the fact that they are rational, sentient beings, susceptible of acquiring ideas of morality, and of reasoning concerning those ideas. Women having, then, the same qualities, have necessarily the same rights. Either no individual of the human species has any true rights, or all have the same; and he or she who votes against the rights of another, whatever may be his or her religion, colour, or sex, has by that fact abjured his own.

It would be difficult to prove that women are incapable of exercising the rights of citizenship. Although liable to become mothers of families, and exposed to other passing indispositions, why may they not exercise rights of which it has never been proposed to deprive those persons who periodically suffer from gout, bronchitis, etc.? Admitting for the moment that there exists in men a superiority of mind, which is not the necessary result of a difference of education (which is by no means proved, but which should be, to permit of women being deprived of a natural right without injustice), this inferiority can only consist in two points. It is said that no woman has made any important discovery in science, or has given any proofs of the possession of genius in arts, literature, etc.; but, on the other hand, it is not pretended that the rights of citizenship should be accorded only to men of genius. It is added that no woman has the same extent of knowledge, the same power of reasoning, as certain men; but what results from that? Only this, that with the exception of a limited number of exceptionally enlightened men, equality is absolute between women and the remainder of the men; that this small class apart, inferiority and superiority are equally divided between the two sexes. But since it would be completely absurd to restrict to this superior class the rights of citizenship and the power of being entrusted with public functions, why should women be excluded any more than those men who are inferior to a great number of women? Lastly, shall it be said that there exists in the minds and hearts of women certain qualities which ought to exclude them from the enjoyment of their natural rights? Let us interrogate the facts. Elizabeth of England, Maria Theresa, the two Catherines of Russia--have they not shown that neither in courage nor in strength of mind are women wanting?

Émilie du Châtelet (1706–1749), mathematician and physicist

Elizabeth possessed all the failings of women. Did these failings work more harm during her reign than resulted from the failings of men during the reign of her father, Henry VIII., or her successor, James I.? Have the lovers of certain empresses exercised a more dangerous influence than the mistresses of Louis XIV., of Louis XV., or even of Henry IV.?

Will it be maintained that Mistress Macaulay would not have expressed her opinions in the House of Commons better than many representatives of the British nation? In dealing with the question of liberty of conscience, would she not have expressed more elevated principles than those of Pitt, as well as more powerful reasoning? Although as great an enthusiast on behalf of liberty as Mr. Burke could be on behalf of its opposite, would she, while defending the French Constitution, have made use of such absurd and offensive nonsense as that which this celebrated rhetorician made use of in attacking it? Would not the adopted daughter of Montaigne have better defended the rights of citizens in France, in 1614, than the Councillor Courtin, who was a believer in magic and occult powers? Was not the Princesse des Ursins superior to Chamillard? Could not the Marquise de Chatelet have written equally as well as M. Rouillé? Would Mme. de Lambert have made laws as absurd and as barbarous as those of the "garde des Sceaux," of Armenouville, against Protestants, invaders of domestic privacy, robbers and negroes? In looking back over the list of those who have governed the world, men have scarcely the right to be so very uplifted.

Anne Marie de La Trémoille, Princesse des Ursins (1642–1722)

Women are superior to men in the gentle and domestic virtues; they, as well as men, know how to love liberty, although they do not participate in all its advantages; and in republics they have been known to sacrifice themselves for it. They have shown that they possess the virtues of citizens whenever chance or civil disasters have brought them upon a scene from which they have been shut out by the pride and the tyranny of men in all nations.

It has been said that women, in spite of much ability, of much sagacity, and of a power of reasoning carried to a degree equalling that of subtle dialecticians, yet are never governed by what is called "reason."

This observation is not correct. Women are not governed, it is true, by the reason (and experience) of men; they are governed by their own reason (and experience).

Their interests not being the same (as those of men) by the fault of the law, the same things not having the same importance for them as for men, they may, without failing in rational conduct, govern themselves by different principles, and tend towards a different result. It is as reasonable for a woman to concern herself respecting her personal attractions as it was for Demosthenes to cultivate his voice and his gestures.

It is said that women, although superior in some respects to man--more gentle, more sensitive, less subject to those vices which proceed from egotism and hardness of heart--yet do not really possess the sentiment of justice; that they obey rather their feelings than their conscience. This observation is more correct, but it proves nothing; it is not nature, it is education, it is social existence which produces this difference.

Neither the one nor the other has habituated women to the idea of what is just, but only to the idea of what is "honnête," or respectable. Excluded from public affairs, from all those things which are judged of according to rigorous ideas of justice, or according to positive laws, the things with which they are occupied and which are affected by them are precisely those which are regulated by natural feelings of honesty (or, rather, propriety) and of sentiment. It is, then, unjust to allege as an excuse for continuing to refuse to women the enjoyment of all their natural rights motives which have only a kind of reality because women lack the experience which comes from the exercise of these rights.

If reasons such as these are to be admitted against women, it will become necessary to deprive of the rights of citizenship that portion of the people who, devoted to constant labour, can neither acquire knowledge nor exercise their reason; and thus, little by little, only those persons would be permitted to be citizens who had completed a course of legal study. If such principles are admitted, we must, as a natural consequence, renounce the idea of a liberal constitution. The various aristocracies have only had such principles as these for foundation or excuse. The etymology of the word is a sufficient proof of this.

Neither can the subjection of wives to their husbands be alleged against their claims, since it would be possible in the same statute to destroy this tyranny of the civil law. The existence of one injustice can never be accepted as a reason for committing another.

There remain, then, only two objections to discuss. And, in truth, these can only oppose motives of expediency against the admission of women to the right of voting; which motives can never be upheld as a bar to the exercise of true justice. The contrary maxim has only too often served as the pretext and excuse of tyrants; it is in the name of expediency that commerce and industry groan in chains; and that Africa remains afflicted with slavery: it was in the name of public expediency that the Bastille was crowded; that the censorship of the press was instituted; that accused persons were not allowed to communicate with their advisers; that torture was resorted to. Nevertheless, we will discuss these objections, so as to leave nothing without reply.

It is necessary, we are warned, to be on guard against the influence exercised by women over men. We reply at once that this, like any other influence, is much more to be feared when not exercised openly; and that, whatever influence may be peculiar to women, if exercised upon more than one individual at a time, will in so far become proportionately lessened. That since, up to this time, women have not been admitted in any country to absolute equality; since their empire has none the less existed everywhere; and since the more women have been degraded by the laws, the more dangerous has their influence been; it does not appear that this remedy of subjection ought to inspire us with much confidence. Is it not probable, on the contrary, that their special empire would diminish if women had less interest in its preservation; if it ceased to be for them their sole means of defence, and of escape from persecution?

If politeness does not permit to men to maintain their opinions against women in society, this politeness, it may be said, is near akin to pride; we yield a victory of no importance; defeat does not humiliate when it is regarded as voluntary. Is it seriously believed that it would be the same in a public discussion on an important topic? Does politeness forbid the bringing of an action at law against a woman?

But, it will be said, this change will be contrary to general expediency, because it will take women away from those duties which nature has reserved for them. This objection scarcely appears to me well founded. Whatever form of constitution may be established, it is certain that in the present state of civilisation among European nations there will never be more than a limited number of citizens required to occupy themselves with public affairs. Women will no more be torn from their homes than agricultural labourers from their ploughs, or artisans from their workshops. And, among the richer classes, we nowhere see women giving themselves up so persistently to domestic affairs that we should fear to distract their attention; and a really serious occupation or interest would take them less away than the frivolous pleasures to which idleness, a want of object in life, and an inferior education have condemned them.

The principal source of this fear is the idea that every person admitted to exercise the rights of citizenship immediately aspires to govern others. This may be true to a certain extent, at a time when the constitution is being established, but the feeling can scarcely prove durable. And so it is scarcely necessary to believe that because women may become members of national assemblies, they would immediately abandon their children, their homes, and their needles. They would only be the better fitted to educate their children and to rear men. It is natural that a woman should suckle her infant; that she should watch over its early childhood. Detained in her home by these cares, and less muscular than the man, it is also natural that she should lead a more retired, a more domestic life. The woman, therefore, as well as the man in a corresponding class of life, would be under the necessity of performing certain duties at certain times according to circumstances. This may be a motive for not giving her the preference in an election, but it cannot be a reason for legal exclusion. Gallantry would doubtless lose by the change, but domestic customs would be improved by equality in this as in other things.

Up to this time the manners of all nations have been more or less brutal and corrupt. I only know of one exception, and that is in favour of the Americans of the United States, who are spread, few in number, over a wide territory. Up to this time, among all nations, legal inequality has existed between men and women; and it would not be difficult to show that, in these two phenomena, the second is one of the causes of the first, because inequality necessarily introduces corruption, and is the most common cause of it, if even it be not the sole cause.

I now demand that opponents should condescend to refute these propositions by other methods than by pleasantries and declamations; above all, that they should show me any natural difference between men and women which may legitimately serve as foundation for the deprivation of a right.

The equality of rights established between men by our new constitution has brought down upon us eloquent declamations and never-ending pleasantries; but up till now no one has been able to oppose to it one single reason, and this is certainly neither from lack of talent nor lack of zeal. I venture to believe that it will be the same with regard to equality of rights between the two sexes. It is sufficiently curious that, in a great number of countries, women have been judged incapable of all public functions yet worthy of royalty; that in France a woman has been able to be regent, and yet that up to 1776 she could not be a milliner or dressmaker ("marchande des modes") in Paris, except under cover of her husband's name;[2] and that, lastly, in our elective assemblies they have accorded to rights of property what they have refused to natural right. Many of our noble deputies owe to ladies the honour of sitting among the representatives of the nation. Why, instead of depriving of this right women who were owners of landed estates, was it not extended to all those who possessed property or were heads of households? Why, if it be found absurd to exercise the right of citizenship by proxy, deprive women of this right, rather than leave them the liberty of exercising it in person?

Catherine the Great (1729–1796), Empress of Russia

[2]Before the suppression of "jurandes," in 1776, women could neither carry on a business of a "marchande des modes" (milliner and dressmaker) nor of any other profession exercised by them, unless they were married, or unless some man lent or sold them his name for that purpose.—Seepreamble of the Edict of 1776.

REMARKS

Marquis de Condorcet, philosopher and advocate for women's rights

Marie de Gournay (1565–1645), early advocate for women's equality

Although I am not aware of any previous translation of the foregoing essay, and do not remember to have seen anywhere any allusion to this first publication on the subject of woman's emancipation, yet I have been struck by the close similarity of the arguments used by J. S. Mill and by those who have succeeded him in the advocacy of women's electoral freedom to those used by the Marquis de Condorcet in this essay. It could not, indeed, well be otherwise, since the fundamental principle of equal rights, and equal claim to protection in the exercise of these rights, must present itself in the same forcible light to any really intelligent person who is truly anxious to lay down just and fair principles of government. That it should be within the reach of every individual of the human race to attain to the power of influencing the Government under which he or she lives, follows inevitably to logical minds, and the only exceptions which can fairly be made are those of the immature and the failures.

The immature, indeed, can scarcely be called exceptions, since maturity succeeds immaturity--the child becomes the adult; and as physical, moral, and intellectual powers are acquired, civil rights must be accorded.

The failures, then, include all those who can with due regard to just principles be entirely excluded; and these are the idiot, who never reaches maturity; the lunatic, who, becoming diseased, loses the mental and moral characteristics of maturity; and the criminal, who is coming more and more to be looked upon as partaking of the character of the idiot and the lunatic. I venture to think, then, that the real issue is narrowing itself down to this: that the opponents of women's emancipation really regard all women either as perpetually immature (to whom they will accord more or less protection, privilege, or even adoration, just as they admire the innocence of childhood), or as the perpetual failures of the race.

If women continue to be excluded from electoral functions, it will be because a majority of men in their secret hearts relegate them to one or other of these classes. But there are, happily, increasing numbers of men who are perfectly aware of, and sympathise with the indignation of women at the affront thus put upon them. These men cannot but feel that the insult thus publicly affixed to all women affects them also. They say: "We are the sons of women, and may in our turn also become fathers of women. Are we, then, sons of slaves, and shall we in turn create slaves to hinder the development and lower the morality of our sons? No! we believe that women ought to be free and equal before the law, so that they may become mothers of free and equal sons and daughters, helping in each other's development, ennobling and no longer enslaving each other."

If the issue narrows down, looked at from first principles, it broadens out indefinitely as the details of its applications and effects come before us. These are wide and far-reaching, and space fails for entering upon them here. But in the struggles of the labouring classes, in the societies for reform of evils, for the spread of improvements, in the work of the County Council, etc., we find that women's help is needed, and that it either cannot be given at all, or is miserably curtailed in its power for good and useful work, because it is not accompanied by the electoral powers which back up men's endeavours. So it must remain till the power of the vote is granted, and so does the Nemesis of injustice and inequality before the law daily work out its revenge.

Suffragettes with Votes for Women placards

A women's suffrage meeting, 19th century

ABOUT THIS EDITION

TITLE

The First Essay on the Political Rights of Women

ORIGINAL TITLE

Sur l'admission des femmes au droit de Cité
(On the Admission of Women to the Rights of Citizenship)

AUTHOR

Marie Jean Antoine Nicolas de Caritat,
Marquis de Condorcet (1743–1794)

ORIGINAL PUBLICATION

1789

TRANSLATOR

Dr. Alice Drysdale Vickery (1844–1929)

TRANSLATION PUBLISHED

Garden City Press Limited, Letchworth, circa 1893

THIS EDITION

Edited and Narrated by Tarah Wheeler

AUDIOBOOK RECORDING

Cedar House Audio

SUBJECTS

Women's Suffrage · Women's Rights · Feminism · Political Philosophy